APOCALYPSE.

SAHIRA MAHESH

ISBN 979-8-89133-963-7

Dedicated to
someone somewhere making an 11:11 wish

Contents

combat

As I ready my armour for war
I strive to be your solace
While all the memories start to roar
I reminisce your embrace

Perhaps even a thousand deaths
Or the anguish I yield
Could not give me adequate strength
To surrender the power you wield

I wish to hear from you
As you have not yet returned
A myriad of words left unsaid
This war has left all within me burned

I am aware that I lit the match
And I beseech you for forgiveness
You are one I could never attack
The distance is nothing but vicious

I need my strongest soldier
As this crusade gets out of hand
Fight by my side; shoulder to shoulder
There is no conflict we cannot withstand

Your absence is the grievous cost of warfare
I covet that my candles and all my prayers
Bring you back and assist me while I repair
All I have left broken and in despair

When the war is over
And our heads hang low
As we bury the casualties six feet below
The last word to let the bystanders know;

We will forever possess our incandescent glow

house of cards

You and I are a house of cards
The rain washes us away like frivolous parts
Of two beautifully tainted hearts
Taught to hold onto love through art

The cigarette that burned through
The walls of the only home I ever knew
Is the one I hold in my hand when I'm blue
Left staring at the stars and my moon

I never found the "good" in our goodbye
How my emotions pour like the rain in mid July
Why I must bury myself in those same eyes
With which you once pierced my soul under the night sky

The wind blew us through yards and yards
We fell apart in a way even the gods
Could not heal what is now forever scarred
You and I tried to build a home out of a house of cards

wilted rose

Loving you was adjacent to breathing
When you almost escaped my lungs
It nearly perished, our invisible string
I had hoped to hold you and stay forever young

I was the rose you forgot to water
I went to war with my own mind for you
Now you watch me wither and wonder
How I walked through a fire that only ever grew

I set myself ablaze
Losing pieces of me to you
And scattered the remains
Losing the only one who was ever true

I longed for you in my darkest times
My inspiration and my muse
I yearned for you when loving was a crime
The one who aided each bruise

With you, I feel like I belong
The stars align ever so perfectly
The flame of "us" burns eternally
Failing to leave behind uncertainty

The story of us is one I will hold onto
Perhaps a treasured keepsake
For the story of me and you
Is one I could never forsake

stranded in spring

Unconditional love
A concept I had only ever heard was
The most addictive and rare drug

I never thought I was fit to love
A soul with all I had and stay; not run
To love someone and give it my all

If I had to perish twice
It would be in the fire of my love for you
And perhaps I would rise from the ashes
No longer the girl everyone else once knew

I would still adore you
With your hands around my neck
It's infuriating how you see past this nervous wreck

I wish to leave your heart unharmed
So I let you take it all out on mine
I would invite you with open arms

You were my first home
The one I never ran from
Instead, in its well-lit halls
I roamed

And as this poem ends
My last words to you;
I love you most ardently
Out of eight billion
My one and only, my muse

typewriter

Use me shamelessly
As and when convenient for you
Then shove me back in the closet
Like an old typewriter, instead of a muse

Leave me alone
Let the dust settle in
But return when you have nowhere else to go
Or a place to call 'home'

When you have but not one soul
Who will sit beside you in the dark
You decide to blow the dust off
And help heal all my broken parts and scars

Now I realise that I am not the one for you
I may be irreplaceable
And cherish everything you do
But in the end it is always her you choose

Even when I fall apart all alone
Willing you to show up for me just this once
You abandon me as though I am nothing
Like the ones before, not that long ago

For once I want to be enough
For you to hold onto and give your love
I want to be the one you care for
Not only when I am about to walk out the door

But alas, as always
You pick the beautiful, untouched typewriter
Instead of this old broken one
Just living for the hope of it all

Forever locked in the closet
Soaking in the dust
Wondering what could have been
If only I was enough

august

The blooming of a cherry blossom
One so beautiful and pure
Reminds me of our young days together
That now seem like folklore

Still ever changing side by side
It's been a while since we've had to hide
Behind a fake smile
We've gotten so used to reading each other's eyes

Perhaps the constant change
Is the reason we sometimes feel estranged
But we always find our way
Back to each other when nothing else remains

The girl curled up in the forest
Dampest of them all
A cold, wet evening in August
From the night before's rainfall

Forever afraid to watch the figure walk away
She holds onto nothingness
Knowingly, yet folds her hands to pray
No sky has ever seemed so grey

But I guess that's what it means
To have a helping hand
Through the nightmares and daydreams
And all the other in-betweens

Because at the end of the day
Everything is temporary, nothing remains intact
Not even gasoline
Go ahead and light up the match

And watch it all burn up into flames
Oh my darling I have done it yet again
From body to ash here goes
My first and last lovely rose

You might think this must be the end
But my beloved, we always make amends
Time and time again
For the other, our rules will forever bend

My destiny is by your side
My fate you will forever remain
Always will I try to be the reason behind your smile
Never the one to cause you any pain

'Tis true at which hour I admiteth
Mine own heart shall ache and breaketh
Because of thee one minute
Yet at each moment healeth
And did beat f'r thee the next

(Translation:
It is true when I admit
My heart will ache and break
Because of you one minute
Yet always heal
And beat for you the next)

repercussions

Standing in the rain
As the droplets caress my face
And collect on my lashes
Falling on the puddles in the grass
Forming tiny little splashes

Standing in the rain
Thoughts flooding my brain
The same question to ponder
"Will I ever be enough?"
I can only wonder

Standing in the rain
Picking through my head
Perhaps you were my one true flaw
One I could never allow myself
To let go of

Standing in the rain
Praying for things to change
But having a miserable hope
For you to escape untouched
I could not bear to watch you face the smoke

aftermath

She lets out a handful of cries
But you disregard the pain in her eyes
And force her to muster up a smile
For which she ruins herself inside

You do not see through her empty words
She always talks, but is never truly heard
Perhaps she always goes back and forth
Trapped in a cage, like a bird

You never noticed the scars on her mind before
But suddenly that is all you worry for
Perhaps earlier it could have avoided a war
The one in her mind that has left her insides sore

One by one
Like gunshots in her heart
They all tore her apart
And to her knees, she dropped
As she could now feel her art

iridescent

You have not realised it yet
I will not be an obstacle for you
I see your future in stone as it sets
And pray it does not leave a haunting bruise

It pains me to know you are oblivious to how I feel
All I have ever wanted is for you to see
But now I wish to be set free
And let you decide what you wish to seek

I will always be by your side
To wipe your tears and see you smile
And to make you happy I would travel miles
I hope one day you learn not to hide

It is venial that you are now gone
And all I have are memories of fond
Even though they leave scars like thorns
Because once upon a time you were my home

I will always have a part of you wherever I go
I hope you find what you have been searching for
But after all the days we have spent
I wish for you to remember me as iridescent

hysteria

Eyes search for weapon of destruction
Target acquired
Self destruct in:
3
2
1

The memories in the air like mist
The tears falling down her face
Her life always manages to twist
Her mind, leaving nothing for her to embrace

But her own knees
On the bathroom floor
Why is she stuck with this disease
Every time it comes back with a little more

All that is left are her ruins
To piece herself back together
As she uses her pain, emptiness as fuel
Relentlessly each time, a storm she weathers

Who does the reflection in the mirror
Belong to, if not her?
Will she forever be a sinner
In the eyes of the ones, her world, she considers?

To her, existing is sin enough
How could she burden anyone
When she fears that the thoughts that occupy her mind
Are the very ones that will lead her to be left behind

Always trying to be enough
Hoping this time it works better than before
But never failing to miss the mark
By just an inch, no two, perhaps four

She has taken it upon herself
To console each soul
That goes through an unbearable chapter
While letting her own self go

Their needs before her own
Forgetting that everyone needs help
She goes through everything alone
And laughs it off, taking another step

'I'm more of the suffer-in-silence type'
Eyes search for weapon of destruction
Target acquired
Self destruct in:
3
2
1

forbidden timeline

My past, present and future
The one I could not have met any sooner
As my heart falls prey to the shooter
Always the one who so carefully sutures

It back together as it bleeds and shatters
Each time I flinch, to you nothing else matters
You leave your own life in order to gather
The pieces of what others have left a disaster

You treat me like your little glass doll
Like at any given moment I would breakdown if I fall
Not knowing I would never let myself get involved
With a puzzle you could never solve

Stacked up brick by brick
Walls of trust, ever so thick
Like the burning of the wick
Of your love, I am an addict

I do not know if you notice how I wrap my fingers
Around your little one
The same way one thinker held the other's
As life failed to offer me that chance

You think of me as a butterfly;

For my wings to break as soon as they're bent
After all the days we've spent
You must know nothing can cause a dent
You have made me unbreakable, my cement

But perhaps it isn't so vile
To be held like I'm fragile
I want nothing but to wait awhile
To watch my brittle wings make you smile

As valuable to me as the oxygen that I breathe
Someone who feels like an undeserved fantasy
I am a whole, yet you complete me
My past, present, future
And everything in between

fated mates

Through the years
Our love turned true
You, a part of me
And I, a part of you

In the wilderness we searched for a home
While we belonged to one another
In more ways than one
And still in silence choose to suffer

I know you and you, me, to be worthy
But we dream of a different life
Where the stars show enough mercy
To pair us together next time

You and I, specs of dust from the same star
Maybe even pieces of the same broken heart
You and I, fated mates with the same scar
Or perhaps god's gift to immortalized art

cherry vine

My right person at the right time
You were who I needed then
Now you seem to deem all my acts a crime
But at last I feel at peace again

Your presence, a privilege I'm sure
Yet I, the villain in your story
You always dreamed of something more
I was not enough even in all my glory

We reminisced the precious month of June
All our favourite moments
The trust ended, my sun was now a moon
The darkness transcended

My right person at the right time
I loved you truthfully so
If only you knew it brought me back to life
The love was for so much more than show

vagrant

The hand that holds you one day
Could be the one who stabs you the next
The most vile and cruel betrayal
A sweet crime you couldn't not expect

Your most prized possession
One you hold ever so close
Could turn into another agonising lesson
Leaving behind an ache that only grows

Now left, a soul without a home
Perhaps you could call me a vagrant
Spending my time with a desire to roam
The halls of our house left vacant

Maybe it's my kismet
For calling another my home
Or it could be a prerequisite
For learning how to live alone

I wonder if betrayal was on your agenda for today
If you woke up and decided to leave
Or maybe along the road, you walked astray
And forgot to mention how I was going to bleed

I have shed tears of blood in vain
Held my knees how I would have held you the same
While the water dripped down my face like rain
Hopelessly calling out your name

Could you be so kind as to respond?

sweet christmas carols

The melody of the sweet Christmas carols
Has been dead to my ears long enough
To know that I shan't be hearing the bells
Christmas time will be a reminder of everything rough

The grinch stole Christmas and you stole my heart
When you gave it back it was much like his
Ten times smaller and fallen apart
Now shrink and weep and shrink is all it ever does

What I wished to stuff were the stockings
Hanging from the fireplace of my heart
Yet my torn chest is where the cotton gets filled
Sewn together so painstakingly you could call it art

They say the holidays are filled undeniably with love
Which has always been a foreign concept to me
I never got the chance to feel it run in my blood
Forever left blaming myself to be the reason they leave

I see the flashing smiles on their faces
While the common folk hang bright lights
If only I could have gone through similar stages
But another year goes by as I pray for my demise

desolate cottage

I like smaller homes
They make me feel less lonely
And not so sad or alone

The tiny little rooms
Just enough to fit me
And all my sacred truths

The walls ever so strong
Playing their role to keep me safe
Never tearing down

The old wooden doors
With rusty antique latches
That look like they've never been opened before

Perhaps 'tis true
Nobody ever seemed to unbolt them
But I never thought that the first would be you

Maybe a little too dark and dusty
There were one too many cobwebs
Until the tenant inside wasn't just me

I hadn't noticed the cracks in the walls
Or the sounds made by the creaking doors
Till you repaired it all as you came along

I shudder as I let you in
Not because I'm afraid of you
But because I do not know where I end and you begin

12:12

We have made it through another year
As the clock strikes twelve your words say it clear
You're still right here
And yet my first response was to shed a tear

Not only have you kissed my healed scars
You have kissed them as my skin tore apart
You have managed to redefine stars
And turn them into everything that's ours

Forever disarming the bombs I set off
Trying to hold us together while I act tough
Allowing myself to ruin the best of us
Till when must I have to keep this up

I torture you by staying away
Keeping to myself isn't something you praise
I must keep my darkness at bay
I cannot let you handle that weight

So eager to get a glimpse of twilight
Not realising the hellfire you're willing to ignite
Please step away from me and into the light
Before I ruin everything in sight

You hold my darkness close
As though it is everything you have looked for
Perhaps I should let you in before
The dark night gets too cold

coffee house

Was it the day you spoke to me before walking out
Or the one right after
When you decided I was not worth the same amount
Of everything you gave her

Always the one you held closest
She was blessed with the privileges I never was
And never even noticed
As I clung onto what she never once lost

I accepted the absence of a love which could have kept me whole
I never thought you would turn into a stranger
A life I deserved was what you stole
As I found the one you truly loved to be her

How long do you think it has been?
For a girl to forget the pain she felt
Not long enough for her to forgive your sins
Or folding the hand she had been dealt

I detest your presence in my past
I am everything I never wished to be
Simply a girl made up of a tragic ache
Who will forever despise thee

Even the blood that seeps from my body
Belonged to you before it ever did me
You are a little too late to grab a cup of coffee
From the same café where you decided to leave me

eclipse

From the day we first interacted
To six years later when we are twin flames
You have always said it's your life I have impacted
And that, my love, is one of the strongest claims

You must know the power you have over me
Is not merely an expendable quality
Rather your treasure you hold onto so senselessly
But you ought to save yourself from pain worth an eternity

It is too late for me to get out of this hell
I was born into darkness like that of an abyss
I am afraid you can no longer dwell
What you call home is now an imperishable eclipse

I would go back in time to when it fell apart
And fix all my broken parts
Especially if it meant we would never forget
The cause of our butterfly effect

You are the finest emotion I have ever felt
Thence you must save yourself before I ruin you as well
Wrecking the places I once dwelt
Is a field in which I unfailingly excel

My angel is worthy of a greater future
Than one filled with agony and torment
I would cross oceans to save you from this hurt
Even if it meant it was you I was fighting against

You are the embodiment of divinity
Henceforth I cannot fly you to inferno
You will find far superior love than my affinity
My pride and joy you belong in seraphic castles of gold

wine red sweater

From summer to autumn then winter and spring
Nightmares of lonely and daydreams of rings
I have yearned for a love that only time can bring
Not once could I feel a truly colourful thing

I have waited patiently for as long as I could
In the shadows of a tree of a tranquil hood
Never procuring the warmth I know I should
Why it must be this torturous I never really understood

I hadn't yet walked a path without looking back
And there are no exceptions other than painful cracks
I never wear colours, any other than black
And taking risks gives me tiny little heart attacks

But for the first time two days ago
I wore my sister's wine red sweater I never thought I'd borrow
Falling has only ever pushed me six feet below
Yet this time I have a feeling I've longed to know

A month since I have met someone new
He makes me feel like a thousand different hues
The world from his eyes has a profoundly unique view
It contrasts between neon, pastels and all the shades of blue

I adore how he is never afraid
Going about life in all his valiant ways
Perhaps he is one of the ones I need to have stayed
And just this once he will be worth all the grenades

He sees over and beyond my past filled with scars
Making me ponder if I belong in his arms
For once I have the hope of a thousand stars
I wonder about everything that could be ours

All he wants is for love to feel better
I wish to give him that and a hundred love letters
This time around, the storm I will weather
For I will never discard my sister's wine red sweater

evergreen

The way my years have gone by
Surrounding myself with shades of black
Is a reflection of who I truly am inside
Perhaps there are one too many cracks

From one to fifteen
And five months ahead
The shadows have been evergreen
Maybe even a protective little shed

What if I do not belong to the darkness of an abyss?
Rather a haven of all the colours I have seemed to miss
What if there is more to life than a preordained hell?
Rather a sanctuary of a love I have so far withheld

What if it was all meant to fall apart?
To gift me another muse for my art
What if nothing ever really went wrong?
And it was all a mere ruse till you came along

Perhaps I am not what I set out to be
I may conceivably ruin everything I touch
Yet this time I hold it ever so gently
The weight not too little or too much

fool in love

I believe in wishes from eyelashes
The joyful little glimpses and flashes
Walking together in between classes
And being each other's perfect matches

I like short love notes and letters
When everywhere he goes he serenades her prayers
How she wears his oversized sweaters
And sips of hot coffee as the weather gets colder

I adore when I am handed yellow flowers
Sitting in the dark watching meteor showers
Or perhaps a mere black sky with tiny stars
And words like kisses on my heart with scars

I enjoy reading poems and proses
The way snowflakes fall on noses
When the protagonist finally proposes
And when I am who you wish to hold closest

I stare in awe as the beautiful stranger walks by
All I can do is muster up a shy yet bright smile while
I wonder if he knows of what goes on in my mind
And is he aware of the tiny backflips inside?

Love is joy, no longer pain
It somehow always stays
When nothing else remains
And a fool in love is never sane

valentine's day

Love;
An emotion that fills you with a thousand more
Something you gift to the ones you adore
Granting them permission to walk in and out the door

A saving grace for the hopeless romantics
A liability to a devotee of the pragmatic
The idea of it makes you entirely frantic
But all it could take is to trace those set of lips

Fifteen years is not a lot at first thought
Yet the earth turned as you stayed distraught
The absence of a love that has been sought
Suffocates you with a feeling of relentless fraught

Nothing fills the empty void made by the dearth
Irrelevant is how each time you take a new birth
To be better than the last and realise your worth
Could not be measured with the weight of empty words

Yet this year round everything is different
You cannot choose to be ignorant
The arrival of a destined one is imminent
Make use of what is left of your innocence

Valentine's day is in an hour
And you will finally have a memory that isn't sour
Or leaves you blaming the fault in your stars
Instead of the standard chocolates and flowers

yellow dress

The little girl in a yellow dress
The one on the swing set who gets afraid less
As whispers of the wind caress her perfect braids
And a father who won't realise as her childhood fades

She jumps from one swing to another
And my heart skips a beat as I wish to wave at her
Bitterly reminded that she is everything I wish I were
But I was the little girl too wise beyond her years

That little girl takes all the courageous risks
While this little girl wondered which fragment to fix
Out of the millions the cruel world left her in
She can barely piece them back together; let alone stack them
like bricks

That little girl has no clue of what pain feels like
While this little girl cried herself to sleep every night
Praying for better days or better yet, her own demise
The bloodthirsty took the life out of her eyes

That little girl has a home still intact
While this little girl couldn't possibly know the fact
Of which was the first ever crack
That turned her world from yellow to black

forevermore

The blinding light fades into a weak glimmer
I raise my white flag as I bow to surrender
Seconds before my last breath, it seems to occur
That you and I are two souls eternally bound to one another

The walls of my home came crumbling down
I sacrificed all of me to save our barren hometown
Yet all that is left of it are the ruins of a battleground

Oh how I long to hold your hand once more
Be the face you search the crowd for
Our eyes meet with a love lasting forevermore
To do it all over again one last time, mi amor!
Mon amour! Amore mio!

My love, remember all my selfish whims
But do not forget I was by your side
Through all your losses and wins
And how you felt at home at the touch of my skin

anchor

Our transparent lives now ever so opaque
Every moment I lie awake
Reminders of you having walked astray
My fierce anchor to heartache

Breaking the chains and leaving you behind
Was a sin of the most unforgivable kind
A soul such as yours, my rarest find
But holding on meant losing my mind

My hands forever glued to the wheel
Looking back your presence seems unreal
Perhaps all the memories I tried to conceal
Kept me a step away from life's ordeal

Our volatile nature, once calm
Tampered with the harmony
Our timeless bomb disarmed
Forevermore victims of larceny

seconds fleeting

Moments once gone live as memories forever
They beat in our hearts like timeless treasures
The bittersweet worth pain and the pleasure
Moments once gone reminisced beyond measures

Every second fleets
Into lost time, never to return
As every heart beats
Lesser and lesser left to discern

Memories filled with pleasure and misery
Hearts that feel as deep as the seas
All fun and games till two turned to three
Left on my lonesome with nothing but the breeze

persephone

Oh my sweet Persephone
Yet again, you have left me
Filled with blades of melancholy
Sharper than those of the grass beneath your feet

Oh my sweet Persephone
I know of nothing but the despair
Of yearning the locks of your satiny hair
Between the fractures of my fingers unjustly kissed by air

Oh my sweet Persephone
Why must our circumstances be so unkind?
That I only kiss your lips when I close my eyes
If only our souls could be forever entwined

Oh my sweet Persephone
How am I to explain to you my dismay
And I crave your touch the longer you are away
My heart darkens while through fields of gold, yours sways

Oh my sweet Persephone
The King of the Dead I am for sure
Yet not a single soul to pass by my door
Could stand as formidably pure as yours

Oh my sweet Persephone
Through all my years in each realm
You alone had the power to overwhelm
With your beauty and charm, the Ruler of Hell himself

Oh my sweet Persephone
How I wish you would return to your king
My love I have seen the loneliest of springs
And know my queen shall feel at home embraced in my wings

hades

Oh my vilified king
Never a one could recognise your agony
Not even a god above the clouds or under the seas
So here I stand by your side as your queen

Oh my vilified king
Leaving worlds beyond repair
The one who could cause more than just a flare
Holds me so tenderly with warm eyes and a dazed stare

Oh my vilified king
I wonder when they will all realise
You were the answer to all my helpless cries
I was not taken from my mother rather chosen to arise

Oh my vilified king
The flowers in my hand turn to clay
As I, too, feel your pain while you wish for me to stay
How heavenly it must be to be cradled in your arms again

Oh my vilified king
You knew my heart always wished for more
Now the crown you share with me, I adore
Tell me you feel in my absence what I do in yours

Oh my vilified king
I long to see my little nymphs and elves
And I know frailty against the gods far too well
But perhaps a true curse would be more cruel than six in
twelve

Oh my vilified king
With the euphonious melodies I sing
The brightest of springs to your realm I will bring
Your love could not be matched by a thousand rings

silent tune

A foolish child
All she could be
A reckless life
The only one she could lead

Stronger for the ones she loved
Untainted confidence and a smile
But the tears fall once the curtain is up
She's been broken longer than a little while

No one to turn to
Not a soul in sight
Crying to the same tune
Every hopeless night

A sworn promise to let the agony fade
But her heart aches and turns blue
She waits patiently for a knight's aid
Perhaps she wasn't the fearless girl
You though you knew

phoenix

Your words set me on fire
I pace across the room
You have always been a liar
Your mouth brings me closer to eternal doom

One moment I am a goddess
I am your most excellent companion
The next, I am the cause of all your distress
A mere tool for you to establish dominion

From the ashes I rise to power
Or maybe someone else you seem to hate
Your desires change by the hour
My wings unable to hold this weight

I wish to free myself of these shackles
And the shadow of you
I do not dream of your riches and castles
If they mean paying such dues

symphony

Love hard and love loud
And love loudly is what she did
Bold enough to read her poetry aloud
While her truth, she never hid

Some say, a heart of gold she had
Others prefer staying silent
It was a love for reason she lacked
But it was her love that meant madness

Worn out after bleeding love like water
She seems to wish to settle down
Who would think to incarcerate her
But the chosen one would give her the crown

Now she wished to clasp but one
The muse to her poetry
Her stars, moon and sun
The Beethoven to her symphony

chaos

chaos
A broken home built on shattered dreams
Two little girls held by the seams
A mother driven by emotion, a father by esteem
How long before one of them leaves

chaos
A not-so-little girl looking for the right one to call home
The world tearing down her relentless hope
Afraid of what people might think so she foresees
A daily reminder of the pain she has not yet seen

chaos
She learns to feel comfortable in it
Moreover, she thrives in the depths of it
However, she runs farthest away from it
Furthermore, she comes crawling back at the first sight of
peace to it

chaos
In every body she holds close
In every face she calls home
In every memory she struggles not to let go
In every tainted smile she comes across

chaos
It exists inside the one she loves most
Inside the one she still longs for
It exists in the fractures of her fingers
And in the raven-coloured locks of her hair

chaos
She stopped looking for a face for comfort
As it was chaos all along-
The place she wished to call her humble abode
The first and only home to which she belonged.

chaos
It hides in the corner of her room at night
Finds solace in the darkness of her eyes
Like a skin walker, it roams disguised
It preys on her mind and plots her demise

coffin heart

I mourn the loss of my beloved
I yearn for your gentle touch
My naivety is the prey you hunted
Woefully, the cruel world is such

Your palace walls built far too high
For a girl of my stature to reach
So you wished to say your goodbye
Leaving my innocence breached

At last I sip your pretty poison
As I anticipate its effect
I hammer the last nail in the coffin
And abandon the last of the wrecked

echoes

Struggling and gasping for air
Overwhelmed by emotions
Is this another nightmare
Or a path that will leave her broken

Living for anyone but herself
Her dreams and hopes shattered
Just another doll on your shelf
A certified people pleaser

Deserted on the island of misery
Stranded alone in the season of war
But not many throughout history
Hear the echoes of a doleful heart

siren

My voice invites you close
As do my eyes, lips and charm
Hear my deepest pleasures and woes
All but who I truly am

I am whom you wish to forever possess
The lady of your wildest dreams
I am the paragon of a damsel in distress
Till you hear my enchanting screams

My soulless heart is yours for the taking
I seem to have belonged to most
But do not be inanely mistaken
They, too, nothing but lost

Wish to hold me dearest to your heart
No caution towards your own
I couldn't express the innocence you impart
So I return to my deceitful home

ad astra

To the stars and beyond
She, a wizard of the truest kind
Wielding her enchanted wand
And even so, her powerful mind

Lighting fires that will not be dimmed
Struck the match with her own two hands
Leaving this world a better place to live
The traces entrenching deep into the sand

Admiring the countless ways to create
Hurricanes of the tiniest whirlwinds
Thunder of the lightest drizzles
And blossoming love of raging hatred

I adore her from afar
As I learn to stand tall and stay strong
Through the wounds and scars
To the stars and beyond

thorns & roses

The words that slip through your lips
Taste like temptingly sweet honey
But how long before your kisses
Turn completely rotten and bloody

Your embrace like a warm glove
On a cold October evening
Then a thousand vines of thorns
That once felt like roses

Those beautiful brown eyes of yours
A million shades of fall to blame
Who could have possibly known
They trapped this moth to the flame

Another year to reminisce
The girl that was never his
The love I never received
And a heart he left bruised

phantom

A silhouette that never got closer
Perhaps truly a myth
But there has to be so much more
If only I had gotten a better glimpse

I met him every lonely night
He stayed with me when no one else could
He made the stars shine brighter
And loved me when no one else would

I swear I held him in my arms
Nearer than most others
He could do no harm
More than I could say for my past lovers

I treasured him foremostly so
Yet never encountered him in light
I had hoped he was more than a ghost
Or simply a phantom of the night?

burn

Burn me like you did our love
And watch me rise from ashes up above
Not trust, but the lack thereof
You made a phoenix of a precious white dove

History repeats itself yet again
While you know nothing of my pain
A wrecking ball tied to chains
Prepared to destroy all that remains

Leave me once, the joke is on me
Pushing me to fall down on my knees
Leave me twice, I wince as you flee
Scathing me inside out to the third degree

Watch me burn once more
And do it with pleasure
Set fire to the girl you once adored
Now watch as I ignite as the rain pours

daylight

I have walked this ground
Longer than most these brazen bodies
There seems to be no other way out
Than fall as deeply as in Byron's poetry

I watch them make feeble attempts
And lead such foolish lives
Yet stand so close to the life I had dreamt
Would be mine to cherish and thrive

In another world I walk amongst them
And feel no shame in this skin
The one of a killer who himself condemns
This is not whom he should have been

Like an alluringly poisonous moonflower
I flourish on the darkest night
The frivolous mortals know not of my power
Only how I shun the daylight

glimpses of you

Oh my sweet rose
How could you ever choose to go
Please stay to watch your little seed grow

Would you really be okay
Leaving me saying a prayer
As each night a piece of my heart slowly decays?

You have not yet walked me down the aisle
Or been there for the birth of my first child
Please just wait and hold on for me a while

When I wish to see you, I shan't look up above
I need to look at you through my own two eyes my love
Glimpses of you through photographs could never be enough

midnight sun

Drops of tears replaced by rain
My lashes at last able to hold the weight
Of a life without wars and pain
A life with picket fences over pearly gates

The first time your gaze met mine
Was the moment our worlds first collided
Ages since our hearts were last entwined
We were made from the same poison vine

You were the object of all my desires
Yet turned my pouring rain to drought
I beseech you to declare ceasefire
Stop bleeding my beloved rainclouds

In your absence I find my purgatory
Contesting to atone for all my sins
I am left reminiscing our untold story
As I write our eulogy and our final hymns

drizzle

I drowned as all the drops
Could barely do was drizzle
Perhaps this was hope
Or tearing away at myself with my own chisel

I stood in a relentless storm
While they all escaped dry
Was I not worthy of the warmth
Or simply never a child?

My clothes soaked from head to toe
Seeking anything but a locked door
They let me go in a second as though
It was not my name they used to start wars

I lost sight of my virtue
The rain washed it away
Along with the stars I drew
All of me is left to decay

oceans away

You hear your agony and become it
An imposter in your own skin
Yet another person you have been
Yet another life you have lived

Once upon a time there was so much more
To what is now a soul stripped of pure
A child whose laughter was a cure
Oceans away, from heartache he must endure

Bear your quill and create art
Of the bricks aimed at your defenceless heart
You are so much more than broken parts
Your valour is what sets you apart

A warrior is who you were born to be
Fight for the ones who have gone years unseen
Save the tears, ruins and debris
Save yourself from who you could have been

august – II

August; a breath of freshly dampened air
Rain showers wash away your sins and your despair
The ever-so-sweet mist fills itself in the atmosphere
And at last you receive an answer to all your hopeless prayers

August; the time you are awarded your much awaited dues
Each moment feels like the glimpse of a ruse
In every little raindrop and cloudy sky, you find your muse
Especially in the night where the stars reside,
And so does the moon

August; when you wait for the storms so desperately
Every grey sky, a child of the seas
Every forest in sight, effortlessly evergreen
Every pleuvophile, to Zeus and Poseidon, pleads

the first knight

The thrill, over
The pain, long gone
Our story, hardly ended
The love, far from faded
And our hearts, ever so jaded

The war is over at last
You and I are but two souls
Nay, demons, of our pasts
Yet the ones who seek passion thereafter
Will be reduced by the shadow you have cast

And tonight was the very first night
I missed my very first knight
Since the time we let our hearts fight
For a chance to hold onto the light
Of the flame that belong to us from soul ties at first sight

closed doors

With each passing day
Your heart cries
Your smile dwindles away
And the music dies

Strength is a privilege that escaped my fingers
Once a reality, now nothing but a mere dream
I drowned out the hallway murmurs
Somehow they sound like deafening screams

The frailty comes and goes
My heart is a barren land
I once was a withering rose
Now it's those petals I cannot stand

I would ask someone to stay with me
I would ask them to place their hand in mine
But they do not deserve a life of agony
They have already been too kind

death of misery

You had kind, soulful eyes
That held the weight of mountains
Even more so, the veiled sunrise
If only I hadn't hastened our end

The purest, most selfless heart
That which never let go of me
Despite the countless scars
I left behind in my memory

A sturdy, lucid path ahead of you
One not written for the likes of a poetess
This, I couldn't possibly pursue
However, I dreamed of you nonetheless

I wonder if this was a prophecy
My destiny written down to the date
Could it be the death of misery?
Or perhaps death of fate

icarus

I flew high and reached my sun
And crashed and burned till my wings gave out
I hurt who I was simply for the fun
Perhaps I should have taken a different route

I wish I had listened to dearest Apollo
I was warned not to soar
Now as my life is a life left hollow
I pray for something more

Alas, my wings were not worthy
And I failed to make the climb
A painfully impossible journey
That slipped from my reach yet so sublime

Maybe this was meant to be my fate
An inventor's presumptuous son
Blinding glory, an enchantress's mate
Took me before my odyssey begun